About This Book

Title: *My Pet at the Vet*

Step: 1

Word Count: 85

Skills in Focus: All short vowels

Tricky Words: go, help, check, hurt, wrap, paw, cone, have

Ideas For Using This Book

Before Reading:

- **Comprehension:** Look at the title and cover image together. Ask readers what they know about vets. What new things do they think they might learn in this book?
- **Accuracy:** Practice saying the tricky words listed on page 1.
- **Phonemic Awareness:** Look at the title and help students blend the sounds in the words *pet* and *vet.* Have readers listen as you segment the sounds in the word *vet* (/v/, /e/, /t/). Ask readers what the word is. What is the first sound? Middle sound? Ending sound? Repeat with other words found in the text, having readers identify the short vowel sound in each word. Suggested words: *dog, pet, sick, cut, cat, job.*

During Reading:

- Have readers point under each word as they read it.
- **Decoding:** If readers are stuck on a word, help them say each sound and blend the sounds together smoothly. Be sure to point out any short vowel sounds.
- **Comprehension:** Invite students to talk about what new things they are learning about vets while reading. What are they learning that they didn't know before?

After Reading:

Discuss the book. Some ideas for questions:

- Do you have a pet? Have you ever taken your pet to the vet?
- If you could have any pet, what kind of pet would it be?
- What do you still wonder about vets?

My Pet at the Vet

Text by Laura Stickney

Reading Consultant
Deborah MacPhee, PhD
Professor, School of Teaching and Learning
Illinois State University

PICTURE WINDOW BOOKS
a capstone imprint

Pets can get sick.

Sick pets can go to vets.

Vets help pets get well. Vets help cats, dogs, pigs, and rats.

Vets check up on pets.

Pets get meds at vets.

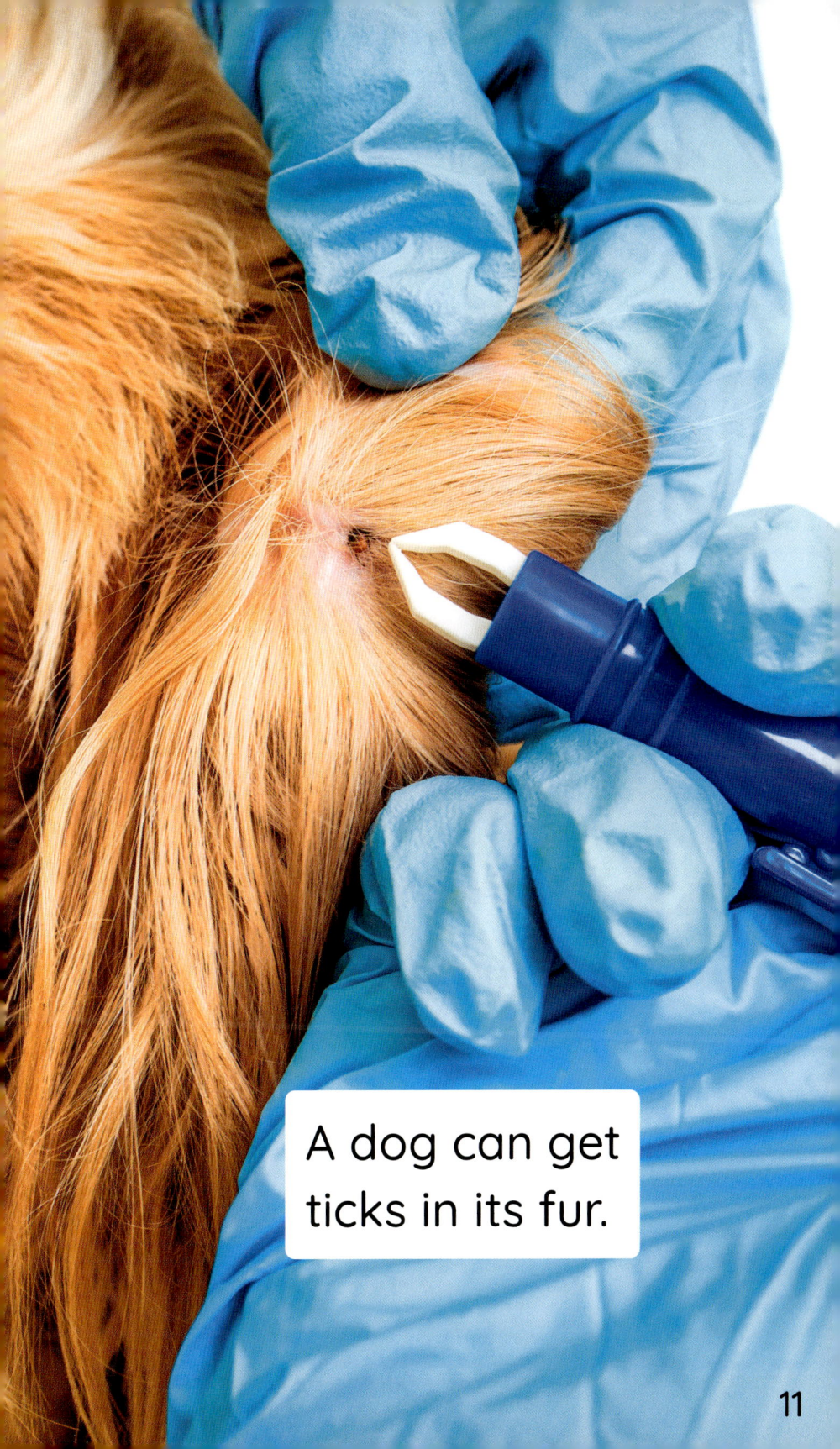

A dog can get ticks in its fur.

Ticks are bad bugs.

Vets pick off ticks.

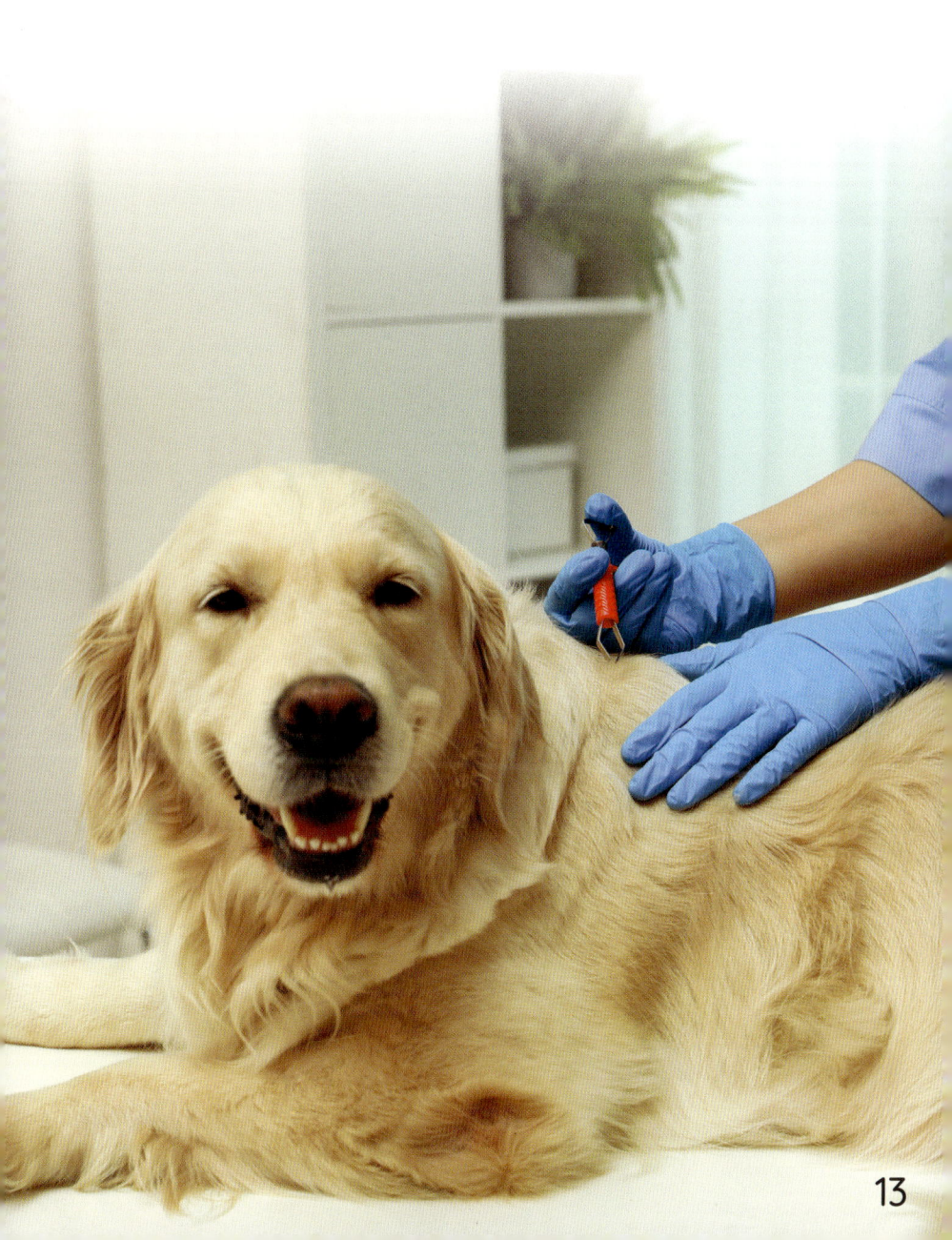

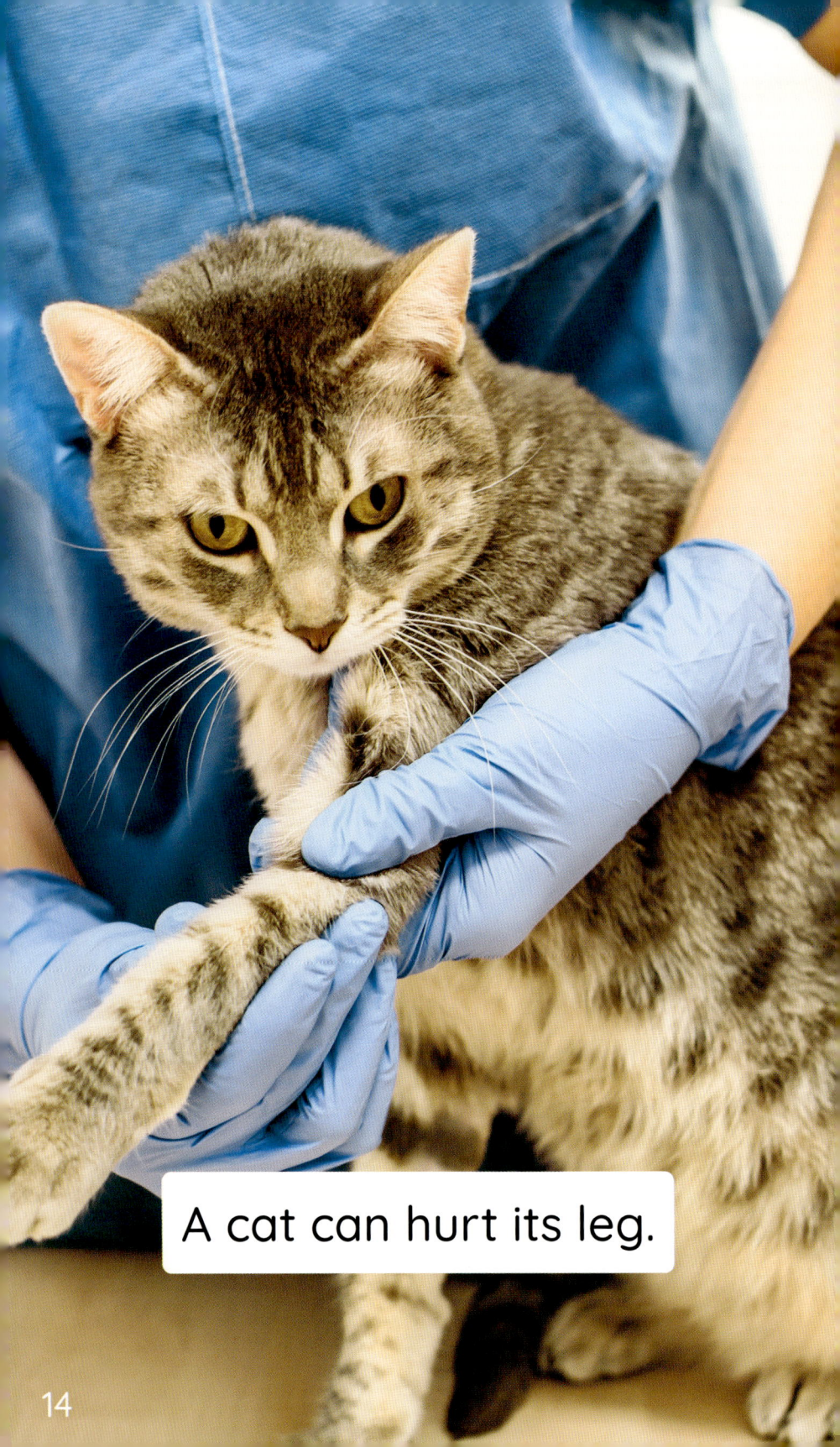

A cat can hurt its leg.

Vets can wrap its leg.

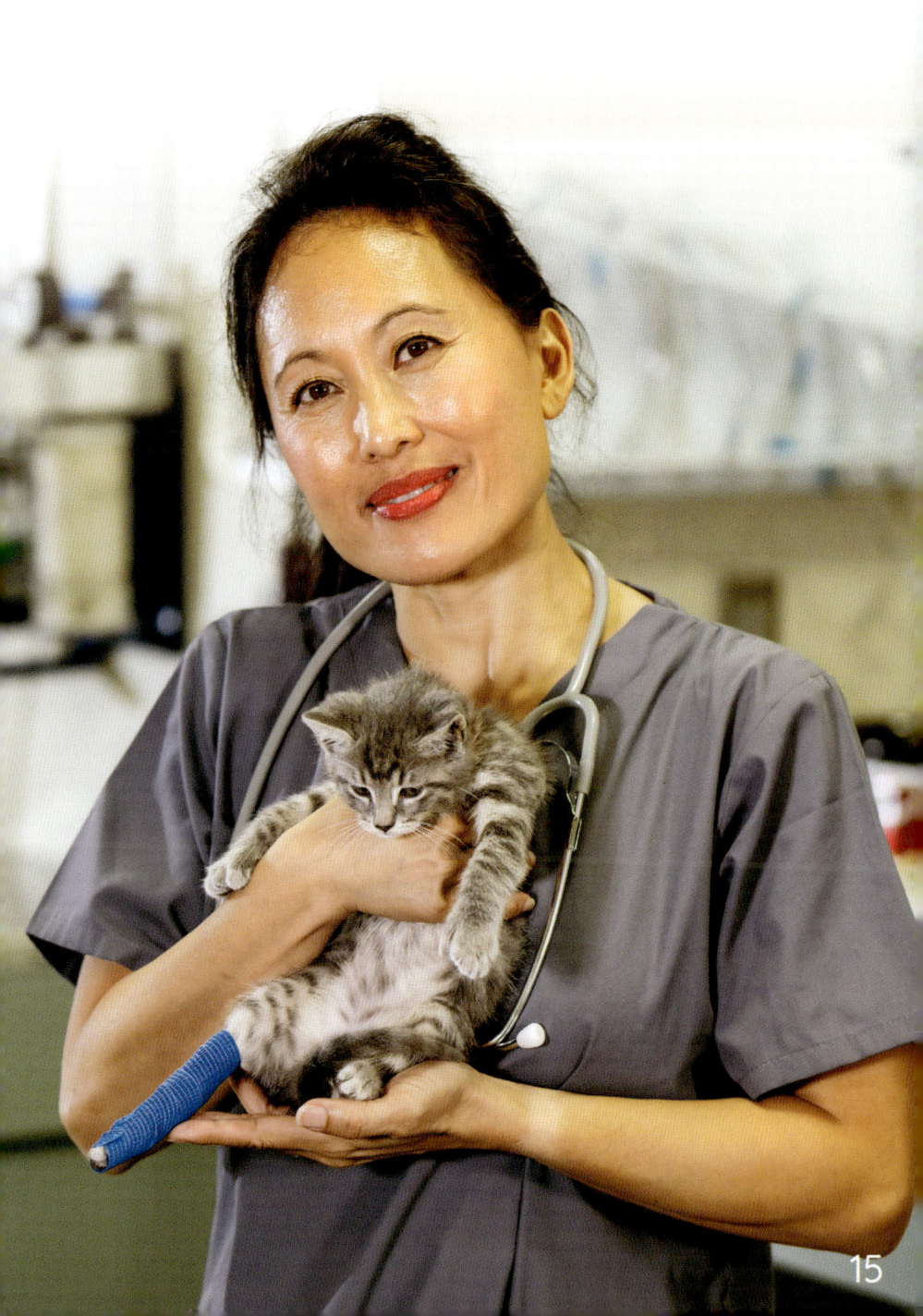

A dog can lick cuts on its paw.

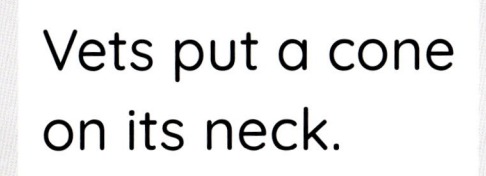

Vets put a cone
on its neck.

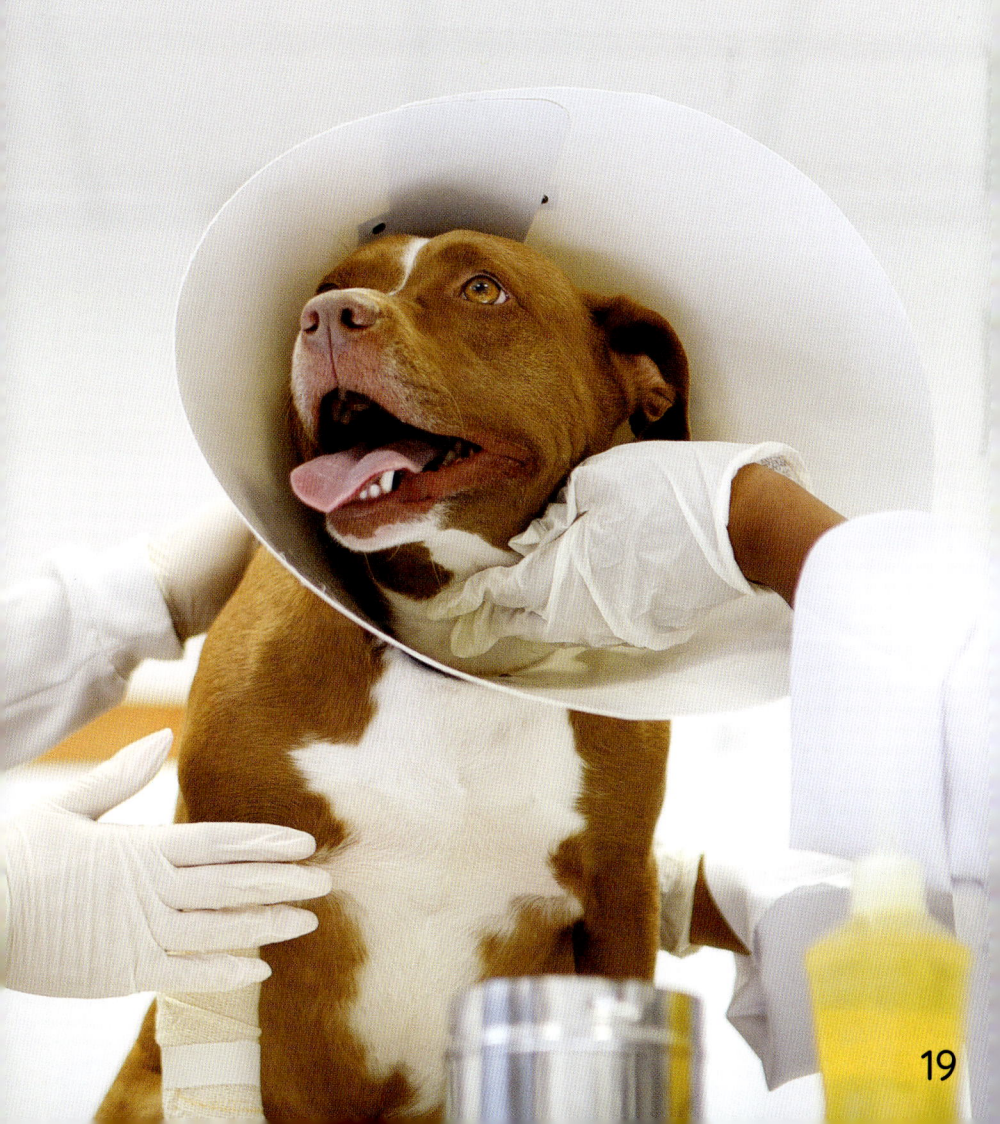

The dog will not lick its cuts.

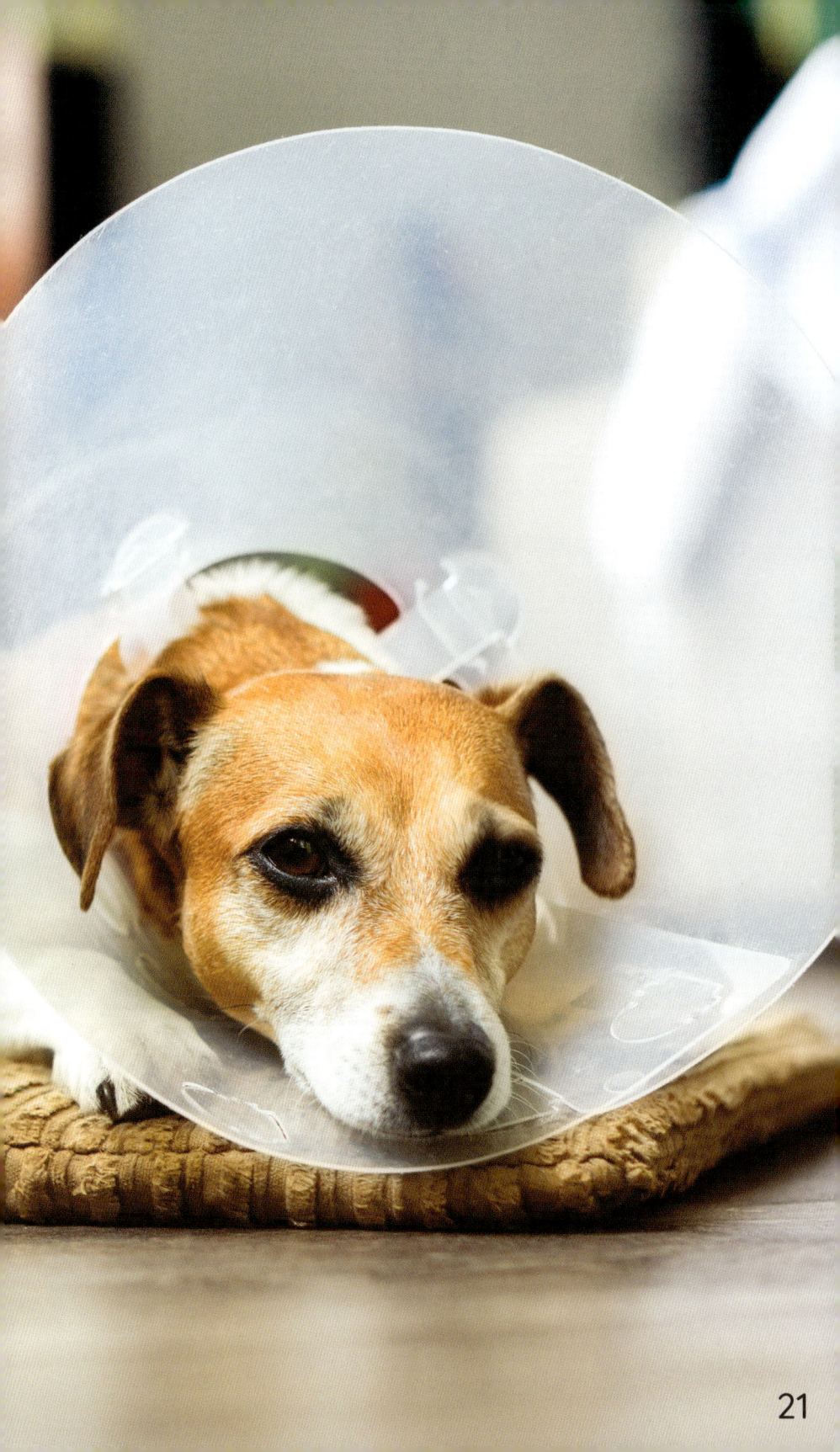

Vets have big jobs!

More Ideas:

Phonemic Awareness Activity

Practicing Short Vowels:
Tell readers to listen as you stretch the sounds of a short vowel word. Starting at your shoulder, move your hand while tapping down your arm (i.e., shoulder-elbow-wrist) as you say each sound slowly. The students will call out the word. Repeat and have students say the sounds with you, moving their hand down their opposite arm as they say the sounds. Blend the sounds together smoothly to make the word. Have readers slide their hand smoothly down their arm as they blend the word. Then have readers finger-trace the short vowel letter in the air.

Suggested words:
- pick
- pet
- dog
- vet
- cut

Extended Learning Activity

A Day in the Life of a Vet:
Ask readers to imagine that they have a job as a vet. Have them think about what their job might be like. What kind of pets would they take care of? Have readers draw a picture of the pets. Then ask them to add labels to their drawing. Challenge them to use words with short vowel sounds in their labels.

Published by Picture Window Books, an imprint of Capstone
1710 Roe Crest Drive, North Mankato, Minnesota 56003
capstonepub.com

Library of Congress Cataloging-in-Publication Data is available
on the Library of Congress website.

ISBN: 9798875226960 (hardback)
ISBN: 9798875229275 (paperback)
ISBN: 9798875229251 (eBook PDF)

Image Credits: iStock: Capuski, 18–19, FatCamera, 22–23, kali9, 1, 15,
Liudmila Chernetska, 13, Prostock-Studio, 5, santypan, 3, SeventyFour,
6–7, standret, cover; Shutterstock: andriano.cz, 10–11, Csaba Deli, 14,
Hyper-Set, 16–17, Iryna Kalamurza, 20–21, Julia Cherk, 4, New Africa,
24, Olya Maximenko, 12, Tatyana Vyc, 8, Zhuravlev Andrey, 9

Printed and bound in China. 6274